Origins of the Earth

Scientists believe that the Earth was formed about 4,600 million years ago. Since that time, its surface has been gradually shaped by different processes.

The Earth was probably formed several million years after a massive explosion took place in space. The explosion created an immense cloud of gas and dust particles. Scientists think that the particles collided with each other, joining together to form huge clumps of melted matter which eventually became the present-day planets.

Scientists believe that the Earth was formed after a huge explosion in space.

It is thought that the newly-formed Earth was incredibly hot, with a sea of molten rock on the surface. About 4,000 million years ago, the Earth slowly began to cool down and separate into different layers (see right). The heaviest matter sank to form the core, or central part, of the Earth, but still remained incredibly hot. The less dense matter formed layers around the core. At the surface, the molten matter cooled down sufficiently to form a solid, rocky crust, which scientists believe was covered with many volcanoes.

Molten rock escaped onto the Earth's surface and cooled to form a crust.

Lower-lying areas filled with water.

The first continents were probably formed from molten rock which flowed onto the surface through volcanoes, cooled on the surface and made the crust thicker. Oceans may have appeared in lower-lying areas, as tiny droplets of water condensed onto the cooling surface from gases escaping through volcanic eruptions. The Earth's first atmosphere was probably formed by these volcanic gases.

The Earth today

Although the Earth's surface appears to be solid and stable, changes are still occurring. The surface is continually altered by different processes which gradually build it up or break it down. Most changes happen far too slowly to be seen and can only be detected by special scientific equipment. It takes millions of years for a mountain range to build up, but a violently erupting volcano or a devastating earthquake can alter the Earth's surface in a few days, hours, or even minutes.

An earthquake lasting about 20 seconds destroyed buildings and killed over 25,000 people in Armenia in 1988.

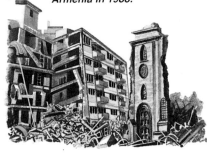

The structure of the Earth

The Earth is shaped roughly like a sphere but is slightly flattened at the north and south poles. It consists of three main layers - the crust, the mantle and the core. Each layer is composed of different types of rocks.

The picture below shows the structure of the Earth, but the layers are not to scale.

The crust forms the outer layer. It is between 6 and 70km (4 and 45 miles) thick.

The layer of the mantle near the surface is solid rock. This layer, together with the crust, is known as the lithosphere, and is about 100km (60 miles) thick.

The asthenosphere is the part of the mantle which lies just below the lithosphere. The asthenosphere is about 100km (62 miles) thick and probably consists of partly molten rock.

Temperatures in the mantle range from 4,000°C (7,200°F) near the core, to 1,000°C (1,800°F) at the top of the asthenosphere.

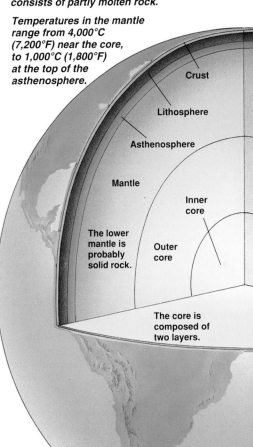

Crust

Lithosphere

Asthenosphere

Mantle

Inner core

The lower mantle is probably solid rock.

Outer core

The core is composed of two layers.

The outer core consists of iron and nickel and is thought to be molten. Temperatures in this layer may be as high as 5,500°C (9,900°F).

Temperatures in the inner core may be greater than 6,000°C (10,800°F). It is solid, due to the intense pressure of all the other layers pushing on it. Scientists think that it is composed mainly of iron.

The moving surface

The crust and the top, solid layer of the mantle make up a layer known as the lithosphere. There are two types of lithosphere. Oceanic lithosphere has oceanic crust, about 6km (4 miles) thick, on its surface. It is mostly covered by sea. The other type is continental lithosphere, which has continental crust, between 35 and 70km (22 and 44 miles) thick on its surface. Most of it is too high to be covered by water, so forms land.

Plates

Although the Earth appears to have a continuous surface, the surface is actually broken into several large pieces which fit together like a gigantic jigsaw. The pieces are called plates and are constantly moving very gradually

against each other. A plate can be made up of either continental or oceanic lithosphere, or is made up of both types of lithosphere. The edges of the plates are called plate boundaries or plate margins. These are the regions where nearly all earthquakes occur and most volcanoes are found.

This shows some of the plates on the Earth's surface, with one of them removed to reveal the interior of the Earth.

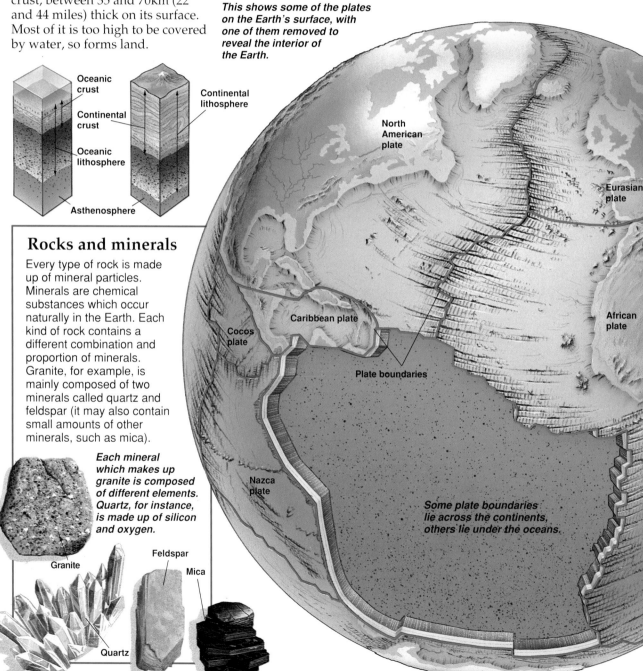

Oceanic crust

Continental crust

Continental lithosphere

Oceanic lithosphere

Asthenosphere

North American plate

Eurasian plate

African plate

Caribbean plate

Cocos plate

Plate boundaries

Nazca plate

Some plate boundaries lie across the continents, others lie under the oceans.

Rocks and minerals

Every type of rock is made up of mineral particles. Minerals are chemical substances which occur naturally in the Earth. Each kind of rock contains a different combination and proportion of minerals. Granite, for example, is mainly composed of two minerals called quartz and feldspar (it may also contain small amounts of other minerals, such as mica).

Each mineral which makes up granite is composed of different elements. Quartz, for instance, is made up of silicon and oxygen.

Granite

Feldspar

Mica

Quartz

Moving plates

The Earth's plates are constantly moving in different ways and directions, although very slowly. They move at an average of 5cm (2in) each year, which is roughly the rate at which your fingernails grow. Because all the plates interlock, the movement of any one plate has a knock-on effect, creating gradual movement of all the surrounding plates.

Evidence of the different ways in which plates move can be seen at plate boundaries (see pages 6-7), but scientists are unsure about what actually makes them move. The knock-on process may well have no starting or finishing point, with just continual movement occurring. However, there are also theories that one type of plate movement may be the "prime mover" - the one that constantly sets off movement of the other plates.

South American plate

Ocean floor

A plate

One type of movement at plate boundaries involves one plate plunging below another. Some scientists think this sets off all the other movements.

At some boundaries, molten rock rises between two plates and hardens onto the plate edges, pushing the plates apart. This may set off all other plate movement.

It is thought that, in addition to whatever sets off the movement, the plates might be kept in motion by gigantic currents of heat circulating within the mantle.

Shifting continents

Scientists believe that since the first crust was formed, movements of the plates have changed the position, shape and size of continents and oceans. Scientists call this process plate tectonics. They have based their ideas on various types of evidence. For instance, the shapes of several present-day continents, such as South America and Africa, look as if they once fitted together. Also, scientists have discovered similarities in the type of rocks and the ages of ancient mountain ranges found on both continents.

1. Scientists think that over 200 million years ago, the landmasses which today form South America and Africa may have been joined.

2. The floor of the Atlantic Ocean would have widened as new rock formed at the plate boundary (see sea-floor spreading, page 6).

3. Today, S. America and Africa are drifting apart at the rate of about 3.5cm (1.5in) each year, because of plate movement.

Movement at plate boundaries

The way in which plates move determines what is found at each boundary. Some plates move apart, some move together and some slide past each other.

Plates moving apart

Areas where two plates are moving apart can be found in certain places along the floor of oceans (see below). They are marked by mountain ranges formed from volcanic rock. These volcanoes are not steep-sided or cone-shaped, but are long continuous ridges with gentle slopes. The ridges are separated by a crack, which marks the boundary between the two plates. The crack opens up as magma (molten rock) from the asthenosphere wells up from beneath. As the magma reaches the surface, it cools and solidifies onto the edges of the plates to form new ocean floor. The magma also pushes the plates further apart. This process, known as sea-floor spreading, is never-ending as the crack is constantly re-opening and the place where this occurs is known as a spreading ridge.

Plates moving together

There are several different types of boundaries where two plates are moving together, and what occurs at each boundary depends on the type of plates involved. At a plate boundary between oceanic and continental lithosphere, the plate with oceanic lithosphere descends beneath the other plate, forming a trench at the surface. The area where this happens is known as a subduction zone. As the plate descends further into the mantle it begins to melt. At these boundaries, mountains are formed on the overlying plate as the crust is squeezed. Some of the mountains are volcanoes, formed as magma rises through the lithosphere.

Oceanic plates

Deep trenches are also formed at boundaries where two plates of oceanic lithosphere are moving together. One of the plates is forced below the other and this plate melts as it descends into the mantle. A line of volcanoes forms on the overriding plate near the boundary as magma rises through the lithosphere.

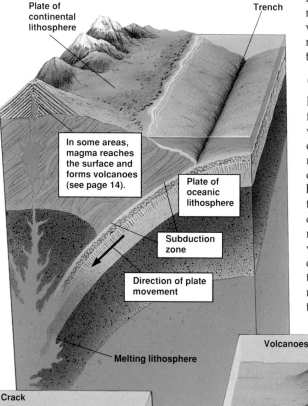

Plate of continental lithosphere

Trench

In some areas, magma reaches the surface and forms volcanoes (see page 14).

Plate of oceanic lithosphere

Subduction zone

Direction of plate movement

Melting lithosphere

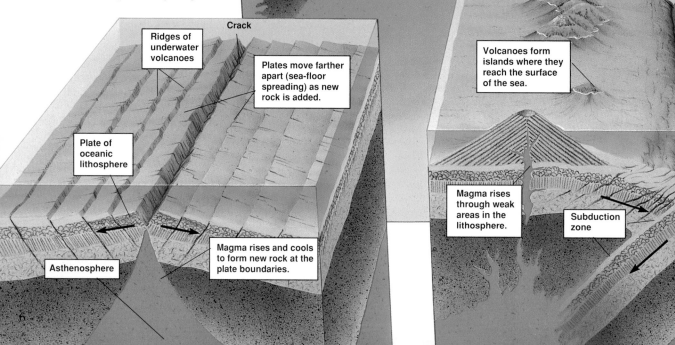

Ridges of underwater volcanoes

Crack

Plates move farther apart (sea-floor spreading) as new rock is added.

Plate of oceanic lithosphere

Asthenosphere

Magma rises and cools to form new rock at the plate boundaries.

Volcanoes

Trench

Volcanoes form islands where they reach the surface of the sea.

Magma rises through weak areas in the lithosphere.

Subduction zone

Continental plates

In regions where two plates carrying continental lithosphere collide head-on with each other, high mountain ranges are formed. At the boundary, the continental crust on both plates is compressed, cracks and crumples up with the pressure of the moving plates. As the plates continue to move together the mountain range becomes higher because the whole area is uplifted.

Ocean trenches

The trenches which occur at boundaries are the deepest places found on the Earth's surface. The Marianas Trench in the Pacific Ocean is believed to be the deepest, reaching 10,916m (35,839ft) below sea level. This is greater than Mount Everest, the world's highest mountain on land at 8846m (29,022ft), rises above sea level.

Deep-sea submersibles are used to explore ocean trenches.

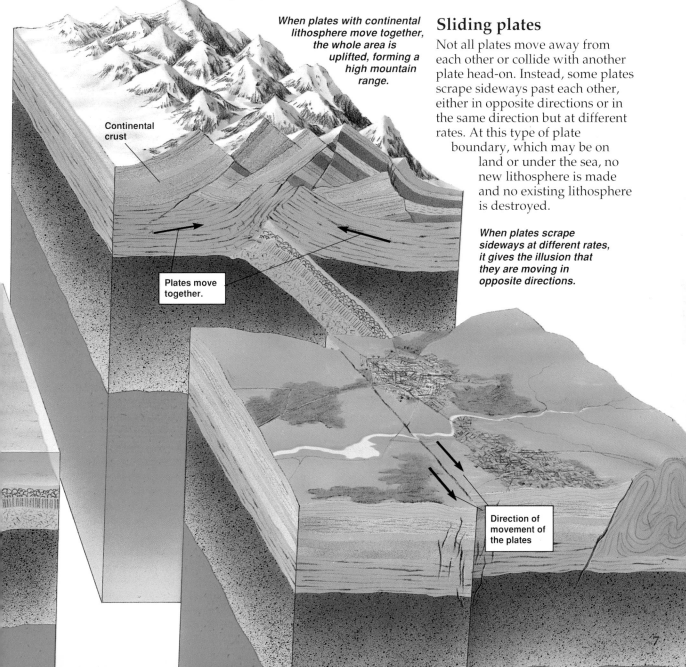

When plates with continental lithosphere move together, the whole area is uplifted, forming a high mountain range.

Continental crust

Plates move together.

Sliding plates

Not all plates move away from each other or collide with another plate head-on. Instead, some plates scrape sideways past each other, either in opposite directions or in the same direction but at different rates. At this type of plate boundary, which may be on land or under the sea, no new lithosphere is made and no existing lithosphere is destroyed.

When plates scrape sideways at different rates, it gives the illusion that they are moving in opposite directions.

Direction of movement of the plates

How earthquakes happen

Earthquakes occur at cracks in the Earth's crust called faults. Faults are created because rock  is brittle and breaks when great stress (stretching, squeezing or twisting) is exerted upon it. Stress builds up in areas of the crust because of the gradual movement of the Earth's plates.

Sometimes, faults can be seen on an exposed rock face.

Earthquakes happen when stress has built up in an area of rock to such an extent that sudden movement occurs. This movement can create a new fault as the rock breaks at the weakest point, or the movement causes the rock to slip along an existing fault. When this happens, an enormous amount of energy is given out as the stress is released. The released energy causes the surrounding rock to vibrate, which creates an earthquake. The actual point where the rock first slips or breaks, causing an earthquake, is called the focus. The place on the Earth's surface immediately above the focus is called the epicentre*.

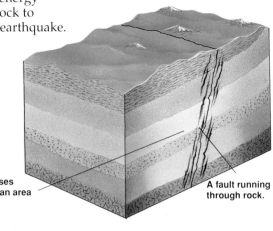

Plate movement causes stress to build up in an area of rock.

A fault running through rock.

The rock is continually bent and twisted out of shape, until it eventually slips or breaks and the built-up energy is released.

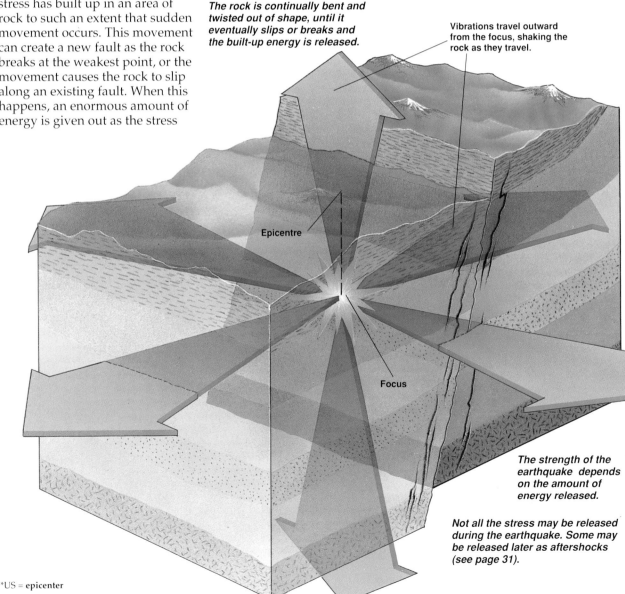

Vibrations travel outward from the focus, shaking the rock as they travel.

Epicentre

Focus

The strength of the earthquake depends on the amount of energy released.

Not all the stress may be released during the earthquake. Some may be released later as aftershocks (see page 31).

*US = epicenter

Bending "rocks"

It is easy to imagine the effect of stress on an area of rock at a fault by using two foam sponges to simulate the rock. Hold the sponges side by side and imagine the fault is where they touch each other. Slowly, try to slide the sponges in opposite directions past each other, as if one part of the rock is being pushed or pulled one way, and the other part the other way. They will not slide smoothly, but bend out of shape instead, until the pressure becomes too great and they suddenly slip.

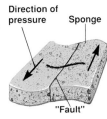

Direction of pressure Sponge

"Fault"

To help you see the bending effect, draw a line across the sponges.

Fault zones

There are many faults throughout the lithosphere. They lie at different angles and may not reach the surface. Most faults are old and inactive and no movement has occurred along them for millions of years. Most movement occurs along faults found at or near plate boundaries, where build up of stress is greatest. This movement may be sudden, causing an earthquake, or it may be very gradual. Areas where movement occurs at faults are known as active fault zones.

Gradual movement of a fault is known as fault creep. Evidence of fault creep can sometimes be seen where fences and roads are displaced (moved out of position).

Shock waves

The vibrations of an earthquake travel out through the Earth. Scientists call them shock waves or seismic waves (from the Greek word *seismos* which means "trembling Earth"). Different types of shock waves are sent out from the focus, and each type makes the rock it travels through vibrate in a different way.

The main types of shock waves are called primary and secondary waves. Primary waves, or P-waves, squeeze and stretch the rock they travel through. Secondary waves, or S-waves, move the rock up and down, like a roller coaster, and also sideways at the same time. Other types of shock waves, called surface waves, have other shaking effects. These do not occur in all earthquakes, but when they do occur, they are capable of causing damage far away from the epicentre.

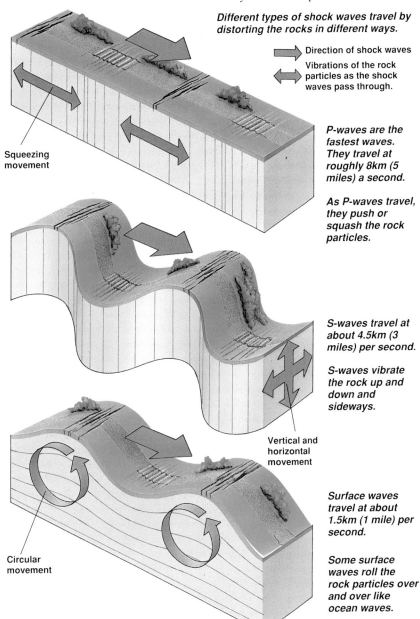

Different types of shock waves travel by distorting the rocks in different ways.

→ Direction of shock waves

↔ Vibrations of the rock particles as the shock waves pass through.

Squeezing movement

P-waves are the fastest waves. They travel at roughly 8km (5 miles) a second.

As P-waves travel, they push or squash the rock particles.

S-waves travel at about 4.5km (3 miles) per second.

S-waves vibrate the rock up and down and sideways.

Vertical and horizontal movement

Circular movement

Surface waves travel at about 1.5km (1 mile) per second.

Some surface waves roll the rock particles over and over like ocean waves.

During an earthquake

Scientists find it difficult to predict precisely when or where an earthquake will occur. Areas at or near plate boundaries are likely to experience most earthquakes as these are the regions where stress continually builds up and many active faults are concentrated. Earthquakes do occasionally occur, though, in regions away from boundaries.

Scientists estimate that over 800,000 earthquakes occur every year. Although most of these earthquakes are not felt by people, they are detected on sensitive monitoring equipment, called seismometers (see page 12).

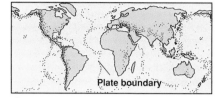
Plate boundary

Areas most prone to earthquakes lie near or along plate boundaries.

Earthquake effects

As an earthquake strikes and the ground begins to tremble, buildings are shaken in all directions, causing them to sway unsteadily. If a large earthquake strikes a town or city, the noise and chaos can be tremendous, as bricks and concrete slabs fall from collapsing walls, roofs and chimneys, and glass flies

around from shattered windows. Cracks in the ground, known as surface fissures, may appear during an earthquake. But, contrary to popular belief, the fissures are seldom big enough to "swallow up" cars or people.

The effects of two earthquakes of similar strength may be very different, depending on where the earthquakes strike. The amount of damage and the risk of casualties depend on many factors, such as the number of people that live in an area and the type of building they live in, also, what the ground is like and whether the earthquake causes hazards such as fires, landslides or huge tidal waves.

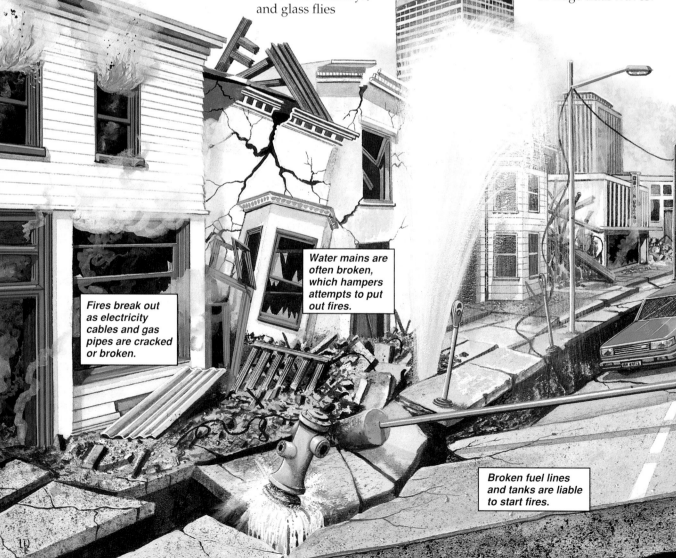

Fires break out as electricity cables and gas pipes are cracked or broken.

Water mains are often broken, which hampers attempts to put out fires.

Broken fuel lines and tanks are liable to start fires.

Liquefaction

Buildings built on solid rock or tightly packed sediments (sand and mud) suffer less damage during an earthquake than those built on loose or wet sediments. If an earthquake strikes where the ground is wet and the sediments are loose, the particles are shaken by the shock waves. Water is forced out of the spaces between them and rises towards the surface, in a process called liquefaction. As the water rises, the ground becomes fluid and unstable.

Buildings which have been specially designed by architects and engineers to withstand earthquakes (see page 30) may have their windows broken and be damaged slightly, but do not collapse.

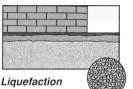
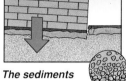

Liquefaction occurs when earthquake shock waves shake wet and loose sediments.

The sediments become tightly-packed, forcing out the water which had separated them.

Buildings tip over as the ground near the surface becomes soggy, like quicksand.

Landslides

Earthquakes trigger landslides which can send colossal amounts of soil and rock hurtling down slopes. They occur when shock waves make sloping ground vibrate, shaking up and loosening the soil and rock beneath. This makes the slope unstable and eventually there is movement as the soil and rock start to slide. Sometimes the top layer of the ground slips as a whole mass, or it may break up and slide as a river of slithering soil and rock, which engulfs everything in its path.

Some walls crack severely, making buildings unsafe.

Bricks, tiles and signs crash onto the street.

What to do during an earthquake

If you were to experience a powerful earthquake, what you should do depends greatly on where you are when it strikes. In earthquake-prone areas, many modern buildings are built to withstand vibrations. If you were in a modern building in one of these areas when an earthquake occurred, it would be advisable to remain inside and get under a sturdy piece of furniture, to protect you from falling objects.

If you are outside, it is probably safest to stay outside and try to get into an open space, away from trees, walls and power lines.

Measuring and monitoring earthquakes

Earthquakes around the world are monitored by seismologists (scientists who study earthquakes). They use instruments called seismometers to register earthquake vibrations. Many seismometers are placed in remote areas and their information is transmitted to central observation stations. Most modern seismometers are electronic. They monitor vibrations digitally (as numbers). Their information is then turned into a visual record of the shock waves, called a seismogram.

An earthquake seismogram

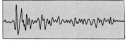

A modern, electronic seismometer

Simple, non-electronic seismometers produce a seismogram using a recording device, such as a pen, attached to a heavy weight. The weight and pen are suspended from a frame. A powered, rotating cylinder is also attached to the frame, which is secured to the ground. As the Earth shakes, the weight and pen remain still, but record the movement as the frame and the cylinder are shaken.

A simple seismometer

During an earthquake, the weight and pen remain still and record the tremors as a seismogram.

Three seismometers, each at a different angle, are usually placed together to monitor vibrations in different directions.

Direction of shaking

Weight and pen

Seismogram

To understand the way in which simple seismometers work, tie a small, heavy weight, such as a pocket-sized plastic bottle full of liquid, to one end of a 1m (40in) length of string. Hold the string at the other end and lift the weight off the floor. If you move your hand rapidly backward and forward, the weight will remain almost stationary. During an earthquake the weight and pen of a seismometer act in this way.

To simulate the earthquake vibrations, move your hand rapidly backward and forward.

Locating earthquakes

Within minutes of an earthquake occurring, observation stations are alerted as seismometers register the arrival of shock waves. At the instant an earthquake occurs, shock waves speed out in all directions from the focus. They travel through and around the Earth and are detected by seismometers. Because different types of shock waves travel at different speeds, it is possible to calculate how far they have travelled and how far away the epicentre is. This is done by measuring the time interval between the arrival of each different type of shock wave. The task of locating the earthquake may then be necessary as information may not be received directly from the affected area. This could be because it is an isolated region, or because its communication

links, such as telephone cables, have been damaged by the earthquake. Information from several different observation stations is needed to locate an earthquake's epicentre.

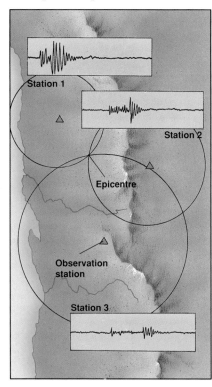

Station 1

Station 2

Epicentre

Observation station

Station 3

Information from three or more stations is needed to pinpoint the exact location of the epicentre. Circles are drawn, which indicate the calculated distance from a station to the epicentre, which is found where the rings intersect.

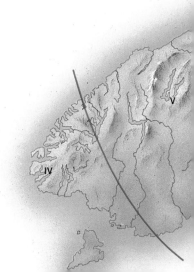

V

IV

Measuring earthquakes

Seismologists measure the size and strength of earthquakes using the Richter scale. The numbers of the scale indicate an earthquake's magnitude, or the amount of energy released at the focus. At each step up the scale, the energy released is roughly 30 times greater than at the previous step. For instance, the energy released by an earthquake measuring 7.5 on the Richter scale is roughly 30 times more than that released by one measuring 6.5 and 900 times more than that released by an earthquake measuring 5.5.

Scientists also record the intensity of an earthquake. This is the amount of shaking which occurs at the surface in different places. It is measured using the Mercalli scale and is written in Roman numerals. It is based on information gathered from eyewitness accounts of the effects of the shaking and the damage caused at different places on the surface.

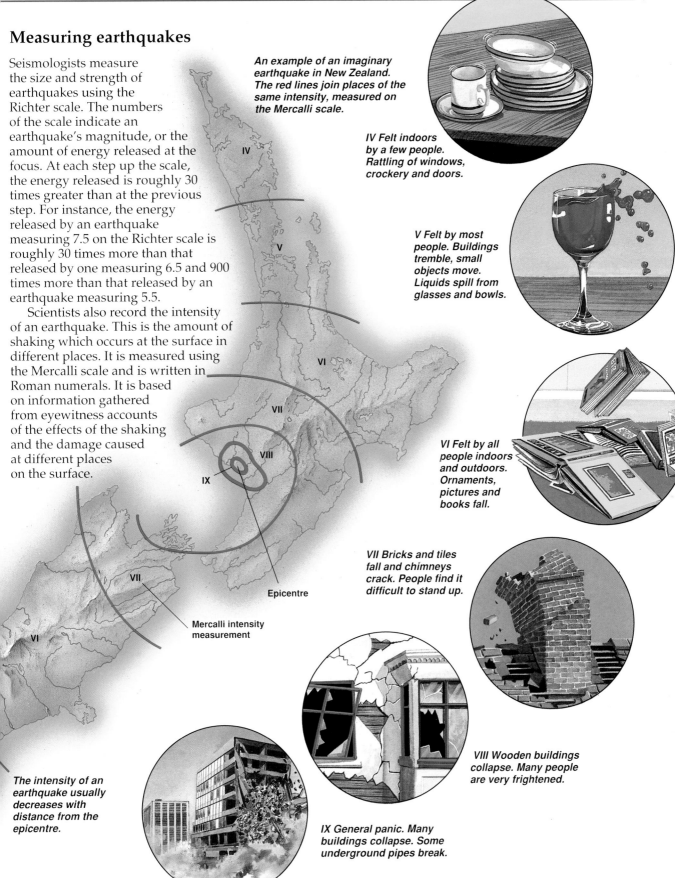

An example of an imaginary earthquake in New Zealand. The red lines join places of the same intensity, measured on the Mercalli scale.

IV Felt indoors by a few people. Rattling of windows, crockery and doors.

V Felt by most people. Buildings tremble, small objects move. Liquids spill from glasses and bowls.

VI Felt by all people indoors and outdoors. Ornaments, pictures and books fall.

VII Bricks and tiles fall and chimneys crack. People find it difficult to stand up.

VIII Wooden buildings collapse. Many people are very frightened.

IX General panic. Many buildings collapse. Some underground pipes break.

The intensity of an earthquake usually decreases with distance from the epicentre.

Epicentre

Mercalli intensity measurement

Volcanoes

The term volcano is used for any opening in the crust through which molten rock (magma), gases and rock fragments erupt (are thrown out). The word is also used for the landforms which gradually build up as material is deposited onto the surface after several eruptions. The material eventually cools to form volcanic rock. Like earthquakes, most volcanoes are found close to plate boundaries. But, just as some earthquakes occur away from boundaries, some volcanoes are also found in the interior of some plates.

Most volcanoes are found close to plate boundaries.

Plate boundary

"Plastic" rock

Scientists usually describe the Earth's asthenosphere as being "plastic". This is because although most of the layer is soft, it is still more solid than liquid. Scientists think that it is composed of solid mineral particles with minute amounts of melted rock (magma) lying between them. Although the temperature within the asthenosphere is high enough to melt most of the minerals found there, in most cases they are prevented from melting by the intense pressure, exerted by the overlying lithosphere.

When a substance is heated, individual atoms begin to vibrate. As the temperature increases, the vibrations increase.

Atom

The movement becomes so vigorous that some of the bonds holding the atoms together are broken and they begin to flow as a liquid.

Pressure

When pressure is applied, the atoms cannot break free to form a liquid, even at very high temperatures.

Plate boundary

Lithosphere

Spreading ridge

Asthenosphere

Spreading ridges

At an underwater boundary where two plates are moving apart mountain ranges of volcanoes are found. These are known as spreading ridges, or mid-ocean ridges. As the two plates move apart, the pressure on the asthenosphere is released. This makes some of the solid mineral particles melt in the region below the boundary, forming new magma, which rises. Much of it solidifies onto the edges of the plates before it reaches the surface, but some reaches the sea floor where it forms volcanoes.

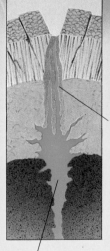

At spreading ridges, as the plates move apart, pressure on the asthenosphere below is reduced and magma forms beneath the boundary.

Solidified magma

Most magma solidifies onto the sides of the plates, but some rises though fractures and reaches the surface to form volcanoes.

Magma beneath the plate boundary

Subduction volcanoes

Volcanoes are also found near boundaries where the plates collide head-on and one plate descends beneath the other. At a depth of 100-200km (60-120 miles), in the area called the subduction zone, the descending plate starts to melt, forming magma. This magma is composed of melted oceanic lithosphere, including sediments which have accumulated on the plate. It also contains water which was taken down with the sediments.

Newly formed magma rises through fractures and erupts onto the surface, forming volcanoes in the overriding plate. These fractures are caused by all the movement of the plates. If the overriding plate is oceanic lithosphere, a line of volcanic islands may be formed if the volcanoes reach the sea's surface.

Magma

Magma is a mushy liquid composed of a mixture of different types of melted minerals and some mineral crystals. Its consistency is rather like melting snow, or slush, which contains water and ice crystals. Magma also contains water and dissolved gases. Scientists think that magma is found mainly in the asthenosphere, but may also come from areas of the lower mantle.

When magma cools, it hardens to form volcanic rock, such as basalt.

When basalt is viewed through a high-powered microscope, the crystals of the different minerals can be seen clearly.

Planetary volcanoes

The Earth is not the only planet in the solar system which has volcanoes. Mars has an enormous volcano, called Olympus Mons, which is 25km (16 miles) high and 600km (370 miles) wide. Scientists believe that Mars has no moving plates, so Olympus Mons could possibly be the result of a hot spot (see below) which existed deep beneath the surface long ago.

Olympus Mons

Subduction zone

At subduction zones, some of the descending plate melts to form magma.

Magma rises through fractures in the overlying rock, forming volcanoes on the surface.

Descending plate

Melting plate

Hot spots

Although most volcanoes are closely connected with movement at plate boundaries, some are found well away from them. These volcanoes are thought to be caused by isolated extra hot areas, known as "hot spots".

Scientists believe that hot spots exist within the asthenosphere and lower mantle. Currents or plumes of heat are thought to rise through the mantle within each hot spot. This extra heat causes the effect of pressure to be overcome and magma forms. As the magma rises, it "burns" its way through the lithosphere, by melting the rock above it as it rises. Volcanoes gradually build up on the surface .

Hot spot

Hot spots are thought to be the cause of volcanoes found far from plate boundaries

Currents of heat rise through the mantle within the hot spot.

Magma forms and rises through the lithosphere to form a volcano.

Volcanic eruptions

Whenever magma rises through the Earth's crust and emerges onto the surface, it is called an eruption. Essentially, a volcano is formed the first time magma erupts onto the surface. Once it has formed, a volcano will continue to erupt for as long as it is supplied with magma, though there may be an interval of tens, hundreds or thousands of years between eruptions.

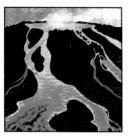

Not all volcanic eruptions are explosive. Sometimes, volcanoes erupt "quietly" with lava pouring out from the volcano.

Rising magma

Magma from the asthenosphere, only rises into the lithosphere when a sufficiently large amount accumulates in a "blob". The process which makes magma rise is similar to that which allows water to drip from a faulty tap* (though the other way up). The water constantly leaks through the washer in the tap, but only forms a drip and falls, once enough has accumulated to make it heavy enough. In a similar way, once sufficient magma has accumulated, it is less dense than the surrounding solid rock, so it rises. Beneath most volcanoes, rising magma collects in an area known as a magma reservoir, or chamber, within or below the crust.

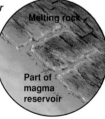

A magma reservoir is enlarged as very hot magma seeps into tiny cracks in the surrounding rock, melting the rock which it touches.

Melting rock

Part of magma reservoir

Beneath a volcano

Enlarged cracks, known as pipes, lead from magma reservoirs. They are filled with old solidified magma which had blocked the pipe after a previous eruption. Some volcanoes have several pipes leading from their magma reservoir, but they may not all reach the surface. The area where a pipe opens onto the surface is called a vent. Vents can be different shapes, such as round openings or long, narrow cracks known as fissures. Some vents lie inside a deep hollow, known as a crater.

Underneath a volcano

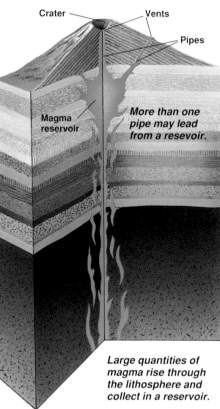

Crater   Vents

Pipes

Magma reservoir

More than one pipe may lead from a resevoir.

Large quantities of magma rise through the lithosphere and collect in a reservoir.

When an eruption occurs, magma escapes along one of the pipes from the magma reservoir and emerges through the vent onto the Earth's surface. Sometimes, magma erupts from a vent on the side of a volcano.

Lava

Magma erupting onto the surface is called lava. It travels from a vent as a river of lava called a lava-flow, which eventually cools and solidifies to form volcanic rock. There are different types of lava, but virtually all lava contains, among other mineral elements, a mixture of silicon and oxygen called silica. The amount of silica in lava determines its viscosity. Non-viscous lava is runny, with a consistency like clear honey. Viscous lava is thick and sticky, like sugary honey. Lava of varying viscosities may emerge during an eruption.

Non-viscous lava is like runny honey.

Viscous lava is like sugary honey.

The shape of a volcano depends greatly on the viscosity of lava. Volcanoes formed from non-viscous lava have gentle slopes, as the lava travels far from the vent before solidifying. They are called shield volcanoes and are found mainly at hot spots and spreading ridges. The lava is mainly composed of basalt.

Viscous lava contains a lot of silica and usually erupts from volcanoes above subduction zones. Since it is so thick, it does not flow far from a vent and usually forms a cone-shaped volcano.

Shield volcanoes are built up from non-viscous lava.

Cone-shaped volcanoes are built up from viscous lava.

*US = faucet

Types of eruptions

Different types of eruptions are classified by the way the lava comes out. This depends greatly on the lava's viscosity and how easily gases trapped within it can escape. Gases escape easily from non-viscous lava, but escape explosively from more viscous lava. As magma nears the surface, the pressure is reduced and the volcanic gases form tiny bubbles within the magma, in the same way as bubbles form in a bottle of fizzy (carbonated) drink as the pressure is reduced when you gently unscrew the lid.

*Different types
of eruptions*

Hawaiian-type eruptions are usually gentle. They occur when the lava is very runny so trapped gases bubble out from it easily. Magma does sometimes spurt out of the vent, forming a lava fountain.

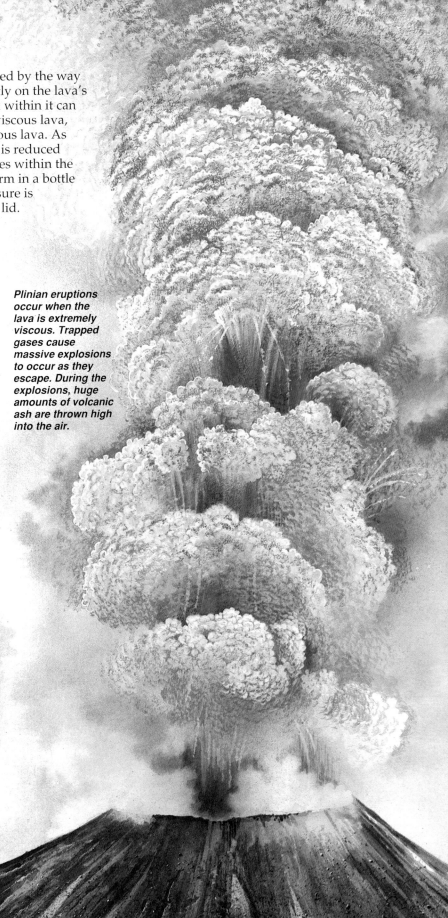

Plinian eruptions occur when the lava is extremely viscous. Trapped gases cause massive explosions to occur as they escape. During the explosions, huge amounts of volcanic ash are thrown high into the air.

Strombolian-type eruptions occur when the lava is slightly more viscous. The trapped gases escape in small explosions which shoot out lumps of molten lava around the vent.

Vulcanian eruptions occur when the lava is even more viscous. The trapped gases escape explosively, blasting solid pieces of rock and large amounts of volcanic ash out of the volcano.

Lava-flows, blocks and bombs

Lava which flows from an erupting volcano destroys the land it engulfs, but rarely causes deaths or injuries. This is because lava moves quite slowly and people have time to move away. Pahoehoe and aa are Hawaiian names given to two different types of lava-flows. Their appearance is mainly due to the way gases escape from the lava as it erupts.

Pahoehoe lava-flows

Pahoehoe (pronounced pa-hoy-hoy) lava-flows usually have a smooth or slightly wrinkled surface. They are formed from non-viscous (runny) lava. As the lava begins to cool, a smooth skin forms on the surface. The interior of the lava-flow remains molten and continues to move, sometimes dragging the cooling surface into rope-like wrinkles, which eventually cool and solidify.

When pahoehoe lava solidifies, its surface may be smooth, or wrinkled like twisted ropes.

When Mount Etna in Sicily erupted in 1992, an aa lava-flow moving at about 3.75m (12ft) per hour, threatened to engulf the village of Zafferana.

The lava destroyed buildings and farmland on the outskirts of the village.

Aa lava-flows

Aa (pronounced ah-ah) lava-flows have a rough, broken surface. They are formed from lava which is slightly more viscous and travels more slowly than pahoehoe lava. As the lava flows, the surface breaks into chunks and the gases escape. The chunks are carried along on the still-molten interior of the flow.

The sides and front end of an aa flow travel rather like the tracks of a tank, with cooled chunks tumbling over the front of the flow and being slowly overrun by the advancing lava. The surface of solidified aa lava is rough and looks like large cinders or burned coal.

Blocks and bombs

The term pyroclasts is used to describe lumps of lava flung into the air by the explosive release of gases during an eruption. Most pyroclasts are made of molten lava which cools and solidifies as it travels through the air. Some pyroclasts, though, are fragments of solidified lava from previous eruptions, which are blasted out from inside and around a volcano's vent.

The largest pyroclasts are known as blocks or bombs. Blocks tend to be angular and bombs are more rounded. Bombs, and smaller pyroclasts known as lapilli, are formed from lava which is molten when it is flung out of a vent. The lava cools and solidifies as it travels through the air.

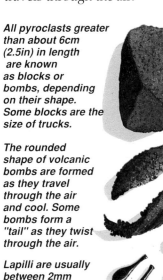

All pyroclasts greater than about 6cm (2.5in) in length are known as blocks or bombs, depending on their shape. Some blocks are the size of trucks.

The rounded shape of volcanic bombs are formed as they travel through the air and cool. Some bombs form a "tail" as they twist through the air.

Lapilli are usually between 2mm (0.1in) and about 6cm (2.5in) long. Drop-shaped lapilli are formed from very runny lava.

Volcanic ash

Volcanic ash consists of tiny pyroclasts which are even smaller than lapilli. During many types of eruption, small explosions scatter ash around a crater, but during some huge eruptions, vast clouds of ash shoot high into the air. The ash may be carried by the wind and may be deposited far away if a strong wind is blowing.

When Mount Pinatubo in the Philippines erupted in 1991, ash shot over 23km (14 miles) into the air.

Burning gases

Pyroclastic flows are fast-moving clouds of hot gas, blocks and ash which sweep down a volcano's slopes during explosive eruptions. Also known by the French name *nuées ardentes* (scorching clouds), pyroclastic flows are formed during large eruptions. The temperatures within them may reach 800°C (1,450°F). Pyroclastic flows plunge down the slopes like avalanches, at speeds as high as 200km/h (120mph), engulfing land, destroying trees and buildings and killing people.

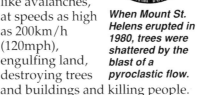

When Mount St. Helens erupted in 1980, trees were shattered by the blast of a pyroclastic flow.

When pyroclastic flows contain more hot gas than ash, scientists call them pyroclastic surges. These are even more powerful than pyroclastic flows. They sweep down a volcano at speeds greater than 320km/h (200mph). When Mount Vesuvius in Italy, erupted in AD79 many of the people in Pompeii and Herculaneum were suffocated as hot, poisonous gases and ash surged through the cities.

Plaster casts made from the hollows of bodies left in the ash in Pompeii, show that many of the victims died protecting themselves from gases and hot ash.

Volcanic mudflows

The summits of many high volcanoes are covered in snow and ice. If such a volcano erupts explosively, volcanic mudflows, or lahars are formed. The snow and ice melt and mix with falling ash and pyroclasts on the ground. Lahars sweep down river valleys on the sides of volcanoes, like fast-moving rivers of hot, wet concrete, burying everything in their path.

When Nevado del Ruiz in Colombia erupted in 1985, a lahar devastated the city of Armero. Over 23,000 people were killed in the disaster.

Volcanic islands

When a volcano forms on the sea floor at a spreading ridge, a subduction zone or a hot spot, it may build up high enough to break through the surface of the sea and form an island.

When volcanoes erupt on the sea bed, magma is prevented from erupting explosively by the pressure of the overlying water. The surface of the lava cools and solidifies to form a skin as it comes into contact with the cold sea water, while the lava inside the skin remains hot and molten for longer. Eventually, the lava solidifies in balloon-shaped forms, known as pillow lava.

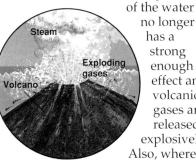

increases in height to just below the surface of the sea, the pressure of the water no longer has a strong enough effect and volcanic gases are released explosively. Also, whereas at depth, the pressure of the water prevents the sea from boiling, nearer the surface, the pressure is less and the sea boils as it comes into contact with the hot lava. This produces huge clouds of steam which rise from the surface.

If a volcano builds up high enough to break through the surface of the sea, it begins to form a volcanic island. Ash and lava produced by repeated eruptions then pile up around the vent and the island gradually builds up and increases in area.

Most underwater eruptions produce layers of lava called pillow lava.

Pillow lava

Layers of solidified pillow lava, formed during many eruptions, build up the slopes of underwater volcanoes. As such a volcano

Island arcs

Curved chains of islands, known as island arcs, are formed where magma rises through fractures in the sea floor above a subduction zone (see page 14). Scientists are not sure why an arc shape is formed, but they think it has something to do with the way plates move or the spherical shape of the Earth. Island arcs, such as Japan, the Aleutian islands and the Philippines, form part of a huge chain of subduction volcanoes around the Pacific Ocean, known as the "Ring of Fire".

The Philippine islands are a volcanic island arc in the "Ring of Fire".

Island arc

A new island

In 1963, fishermen off the coast of Iceland saw smoke rising from the surface of the sea and thought it was a boat on fire. In fact, it wasn't smoke that they were seeing, but ash and steam rising from a volcano which was erupting just below the surface of the sea. As the top of the volcano broke through the surface of the sea, lava and ash began to build up around the vent. During the following four years the volcano continued to erupt and grow, forming an island which was named Surtsey, after Surt, the Nordic giant of fire.

Over a period of several weeks, the volcano built up, undetected, on the sea floor. It was discovered when steam was seen billowing from the surface of the sea.

Once the top of the volcano was just below the surface of the sea, lava, ash and rocks were flung violently out of the vent. The island began to build up gradually.

Once the volcano had grown and the sea could no longer reach the vent, lava fountains and lava-flows continued over a period of several months to build up the island.

Hot spot islands

Volcanic islands, such as the Hawaiian Islands, which occur away from plate boundaries, are thought to be formed above areas of the Earth called hot spots (see page 15). Scientists believe that in relation to the Earth's plates, which are constantly moving, hot spots remain in fixed positions. They think that the movement of the plates over thousands of years carries a volcanic island away from its hot spot. Each volcano is thought to become inactive as it is no longer supplied with magma from its hot spot. Over thousands of years a new volcano forms on the part of the plate now lying above the hot spot. As the process continues over millions of years, a chain of islands is formed.

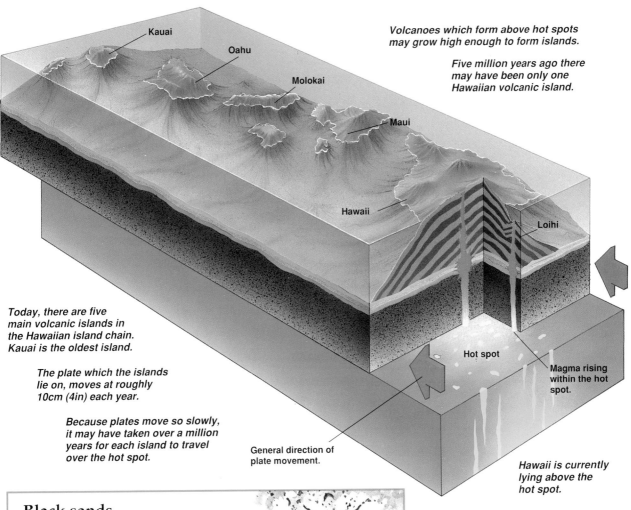

Volcanoes which form above hot spots may grow high enough to form islands.

Five million years ago there may have been only one Hawaiian volcanic island.

Kauai

Oahu

Molokai

Maui

Hawaii

Loihi

Today, there are five main volcanic islands in the Hawaiian island chain. Kauai is the oldest island.

The plate which the islands lie on, moves at roughly 10cm (4in) each year.

Because plates move so slowly, it may have taken over a million years for each island to travel over the hot spot.

General direction of plate movement.

Hot spot

Magma rising within the hot spot.

Hawaii is currently lying above the hot spot.

Black sands

On volcanic islands formed at spreading ridges and hot spots, the sand found on beaches is black. This is because the islands are formed from basalt lava which is black. When a lava-flow travels down from a vent and meets the sea, the surface of the lava is instantly cooled. The sudden change in temperature shatters much of the lava into tiny fragments of sand.

Basalt sand is black because it contains a large amount of dark minerals, such as pyroxene.

An underwater volcano, known as Loihi, is also thought to lie over the hot spot.

If the hot spot theory is correct, the underwater volcano, known as Loihi, lying near the coast of Hawaii, could gradually build up and break through the surface, forming the next island in the Hawaiian chain.

21

Active, dormant and extinct

Volcanologists (scientists who study volcanoes) put volcanoes into categories depending on when they last erupted and whether there is a chance that they could erupt again. The terms active, dormant (sleeping) and extinct (dead) have been used for many years for the different categories, although in recent years volcanologists have redefined the meanings of the active and extinct categories.

Active volcanoes

The term active used to refer to a volcano which was either erupting, or had erupted during recorded history (when someone witnessed an eruption and wrote a detailed account of it).

This is probably what the city of Herculaneum looked like when the Roman writer Pliny wrote an eyewitness account of the eruption of Mount Vesuvius in AD79. His account is thought to be one of the first written records of an eruption.

The period of recorded history varies greatly around the world, so this method of classification is not very scientific. In Hawaii, for instance, the earliest written records are about 200 years old, whereas in Europe some records date back over 2,000 years. Volcanologists now believe that any volcano which has erupted in the last 10,000 years has a chance of erupting again and should be placed in the active category.

Pele, volcano goddess

Although written accounts of eruptions in Hawaii are no older than 200 years, there are many much older legends which may be based on actual eruptions.

Many of the legends are about Pele, the beautiful but temperamental goddess of volcanoes. Whenever she became angry she caused earthquakes as she stamped her feet. She also caused volcanoes to erupt as she dug a "fire pit" in the ground with a magic stick.

Some Hawaiians make offerings to Pele who, they believe, still lives inside Kilauea, an active volcano on Hawaii.

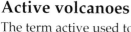

Pliny described the huge cloud which rose above Vesuvius and ash which fell "hotter and thicker" on Pompeii and Herculaneum during the eruption.

Dormant volcanoes

The term dormant refers to any volcano which shows no sign of activity, but which scientists think is likely to erupt again. It is also used to describe a volcano in the updated active category which is not actually erupting at present.

Some dormant volcanoes give off volcanic gases, such as sulphur and carbon dioxide. These gases are formed as magma inside a volcano gradually cools. The gases escape through small vents, called fumaroles.

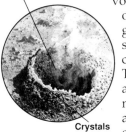

Fumarole

Crystals

Volcanic gases, such as sulphur dioxide, sometimes deposit crystals around the edges of fumaroles.

Dating eruptions

Geologists calculate when eruptions occurred in the past by taking samples from different layers of rock on a volcano. Organic material, such as plants, pollen and seeds, is often trapped within lava or ash during an eruption. By using a process called radiocarbon dating, geologists are able to calculate the age of the organic material in layers of volcanic rock, which in turn gives an indication of when different eruptions took place. They are also able to assess the kind of eruption which took place. Layers of ash, for example, show that an explosive eruption took place.

Samples of volcanic rock show different layers formed during an eruption.

By studying the layers, geologists estimate when an eruption happened.

Extinct volcanoes

A volcano is considered to be extinct if there have been no signs of activity over the last 10,000 years. It is thought to be highly unlikely to erupt in the future. Sometimes, though, a so-called extinct volcano erupts, and has to be moved to the active category.

Ship Rock in New Mexico is part of an extinct volcano. The slopes of the volcano have been eroded (worn away) by wind and rain, to reveal magma which solidified within the volcano's pipe.

Edinburgh Castle in Scotland is built on the remains of a volcano which was active about 340 million years ago. The surrounding slopes of the volcano were worn away by ice during the Ice Age.

There are over 200 extinct volcanoes in the Puy-de-Dôme region in central France. These are probably hot spot volcanoes (see page 21), which were active over the last 2 million years.

El Chichón in Mexico was believed to be extinct until it suddenly erupted in 1982. Scientists have studied the volcano since this eruption and they have now found evidence which shows that the previous eruption was probably only about 1,200 years ago.

Frequency of eruptions

Some volcanoes seem to have a regular time interval between one eruption and the next. Scientists are unsure what causes regular eruptions. Mauna Loa and Kilauea in Hawaii erupt, on average, every two to three years. Mount St. Helens (see page 28) has erupted every 150 years or so. Stromboli, near Sicily, has erupted almost continuously for hundreds of years. Roughly every 15-30 minutes, lava erupts from its vent. Ancient Greek sailors are thought to have navigated their ships by the glow from its crater. It is also said that aircraft used the erupting volcano as a navigational aid during the Second World War.

Small explosions fling lava from a vent on Stromboli every 15-30 minutes or so.

Hot rock

In regions where volcanoes are found, magma rises into the crust and heats rock which is relatively near the surface. In these areas, the rock may contain groundwater which is rain or sea water which has seeped down. If so, this water is heated by the surrounding hot rock.

Water seeps into the rock through fissures or between particles in the rock.

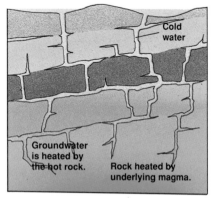

Cold water

Groundwater is heated by the hot rock.

Rock heated by underlying magma.

Hot springs

In volcanic areas, hot water emerges onto the surface as hot springs, or thermal springs. They are formed when groundwater is heated by hot rock. As the water is heated, it becomes less dense, so rises through fissures or cracks and bubbles out onto the surface.

As water passes through the hot rock, chemical reactions take place which change the composition of both the water and some of the minerals in the rock. Some of the minerals in the water are deposited around the edge of hot springs.

Water, heated by hot rocks, bubbles to the surface as hot springs.

Minerals are often deposited around hot springs.

Geysers

A geyser is a jet of hot water and steam which shoots into the air from a vent in the ground. Geysers are found at hot springs where some of the heated groundwater becomes trapped in a network of small fissures and larger cavities beneath the surface. Because the water is trapped, it is heated by the surrounding rock until it boils and forms large amounts of steam. The pressure of the steam forces the water through the constriction and out of the vent, forming a geyser. A geyser continues to erupt until the cavities are empty.

Once a geyser has erupted, groundwater seeps into the cavities and the heating process starts again. Geysers may have several days or weeks between eruptions, but this depends on the time it takes for groundwater to seep into and fill the cavities.

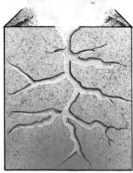

Steam and water

Dome of water

Cavities filled with water

Constriction

Groundwater travels into a network of fissures and cavities. The water is heated by the surrounding rock. The heated water is trapped by a constriction and cannot easily rise to the surface.

As the water begins to boil, pressure builds up in the cavities beneath the surface. The surface of the water lying in the vent is pushed upward to form a dome by the increased pressure .

When the pressure in the cavities becomes so great, the geyser erupts, shooting a jet of steam and water into the air. Groundwater seeps into the empty cavities and the process begins again.

Underwater springs

Scientists have recently discovered that along spreading ridges (see page 14), hot springs emerge through vents in the sea floor. These vents are known as hydrothermal vents and the temperature of the water emerging from them is about 350°C (660°F), compared with 2°C (35°F) in the surrounding sea. Like hot springs on land, they are formed from water, in this case sea water, which has seeped into the rock.

Cold sea water seeps into the sea floor through small fissures. The water is heated by the surrounding rocks so it rises. Hot springs emerge through vents.

Volcanic bird nests

On the volcanic island of Sulawesi, a species of bird called a maleo uses heat given out by warm volcanic sands to incubate its eggs. It is thought that magma, relatively near the surface, keeps the sands at a temperature between 32°C (90° F) and 38°C (100°F). The maleos lay their eggs in holes up to 1m (40in) deep and cover them over with the hot volcanic sand. When the chicks hatch, they dig their way to the surface unaided.

Maleos dig nests in warm volcanic sands. The heat from the sand incubates the eggs, until the chicks are ready to hatch.

Using hot rocks

Geothermal energy is the heat energy in volcanic rocks. It can be used for heating buildings and producing electricity. Heated groundwater is brought to the surface via boreholes which are drilled into hot rock containing water-filled fissures. The heated water is converted into steam which is used to turn turbines to generate electricity.

Engineers are also developing methods of utilizing hot rock in areas where there are no natural fissures. Artifical cracks are created in the hot rock and cold water is pumped down into them. The cold water is heated by the hot rocks and is pumped up to the surface, where it is used to generate electricity.

Electricity is generated using heated water brought to the surface at a geothermal power station.

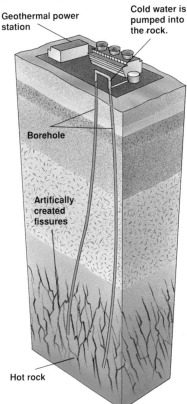

Geothermal power station

Cold water is pumped into the rock.

Borehole

Artifically created fissures

Hot rock

The water is heated by the hot rock and is pumped back up to the generating station through a second borehole.

Black smokers

Some hydrothermal vents are known as black smokers because they emit cloudy, black plumes of hot water. As cold sea water seeps into the sea floor, chemicals in the water react with the rock and dissolve some of its minerals. As the hot spring emerges into the cold sea water, it appears as a dark, cloudy liquid due to tiny mineral grains which are suspended within it. Some of the minerals are deposited around each vent to form a hollow chimney, which may measure 6m (20ft). Unusual species of creatures have been discovered living near black smokers at a depth of 3km (2 miles).

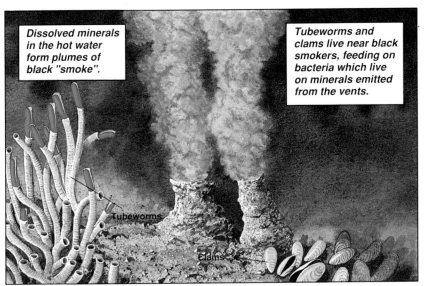

Dissolved minerals in the hot water form plumes of black "smoke".

Tubeworms and clams live near black smokers, feeding on bacteria which live on minerals emitted from the vents.

Tubeworms

Clams

Tsunami

A tsunami is a series of waves which are formed when a large earthquake or volcanic eruption occurs under the sea or on land near a coast. Many tsunami waves are quite small, but they can be massive and may cause flooding and destruction as they surge onto coasts. Tsunami are named after the Japanese word for harbour waves. They are sometimes called tidal waves although they are not caused by the movement of tides.

Massive waves

A tsunami is created when the level of the sea floor is moved up or down along a fault during an earthquake, or when part of a volcano collapses into the sea as it erupts. They are also created when an earthquake or eruption occurs on land near a coast. In all cases, the force of the ground movements causes tsunami waves to form on the surface of the sea as the sea floor rises or falls. Out at sea these waves are no bigger than normal waves, but they travel at a much greater speed. They spread out rapidly in all directions moving at amazing speeds of about 800km/h (500mph).

An underwater earthquake causes the sea floor to rise or fall.

Movement of the sea bed moves the sea above forming small tsunami waves on the sea surface.

Tsunami waves move out rapidly in all directions from the place where they were formed.

Like all waves, as a tsunami wave enters shallow water, its speed decreases, while its height begins to increase. Because the tsunami wave travels so quickly, as it slows down, its height increases dramatically to form a towering wall of water which crashes onto a shore. Some tsunami waves can rise to 30 to 50m (100 to 165ft). Their height depends greatly on the shape of the coast and the depth of the water at the coast. Not all earthquakes and eruptions which occur cause tsunami, and not all tsunami are massive.

Out at sea the tsunami waves are small, but travel very quickly. As the waves approach shallow water they slow down and their height rapidly increases.

Krakatau

In 1883, the volcanic island of Krakatau in Indonesia, erupted explosively. The force of the eruption blasted away about 20km³ (5 cubic miles) of the island and volcanic ash fell over an area of 500,000km² (310, 500 square miles). The blast also caused a massive tsunami. Waves more than 30m (100ft) high engulfed nearby islands and it is estimated that over 36,000 people in coastal villages were killed.

Krakatau today

The outline shows the size of Krakatau before the eruption in 1883.

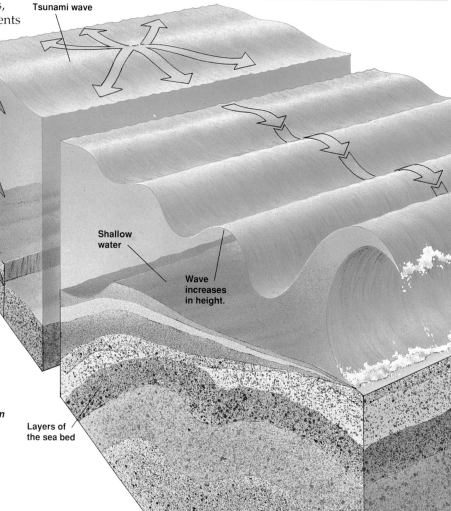

Tsunami wave

Shallow water

Wave increases in height.

Displaced sea bed

Layers of the sea bed

Crossing oceans

Large earthquakes or volcanic eruptions can create tsunami which can travel vast distances across large oceans.

In 1960, an earthquake off the coast of Chile caused a tsunami, which not only devastated areas along the coast of Chile, but also swept 12,500km (7,760 miles) across the Pacific Ocean. The waves struck the island of Hawaii 15 hours later and crashed onto the coast of Japan 22 hours after the original earthquake.

This map shows how tsunami waves, formed by an underwater earthquake near Chile, spread out across the Pacific.

Tsunami waves, 6m (20ft) high surged onto the coast of Japan.

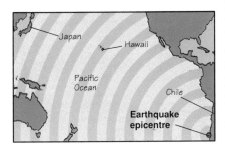

Gigantic tsunami waves smash onto shores.

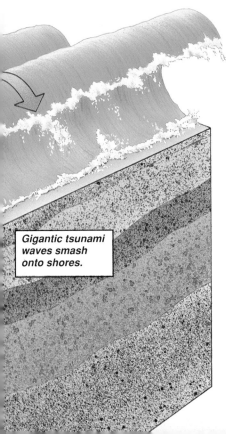

Tsunami warning system

Tsunami are most common around the Pacific Ocean as large earthquakes and eruptions frequently occur there. An International Tsunami Warning Centre has been established in Hawaii to monitor earthquakes around the Pacific Ocean and issue warnings when a tsunami may occur.

When a large earthquake takes place, observation stations around the Pacific locate its epicentre (see page 8) and the information is sent to the warning centre in Hawaii. If the earthquake is thought to be large enough to generate a tsunami, places around the Pacific are alerted and warnings are issued. Tide stations around the coast also monitor the arrival of the tsunami.

Emergency plans

Coastal areas nearest an earthquake or an eruption are most likely to suffer from a tsunami because the waves strike so quickly that there is no time for a warning to be issued. Although there is nothing that can be done to prevent a tsunami, many populated areas around the Pacific have emergency evacuation plans which are brought into action if a tsunami warning is issued. In 1964, for example, an earthquake close to the coast of Alaska, triggered a tsunami which hit several towns. As news of the tsunami spread, people in many coastal areas were warned and evacuated to safe places.

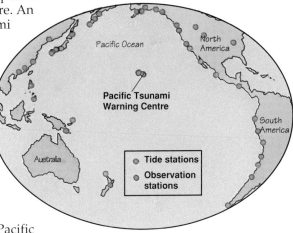

Observation stations and tide stations around the Pacific monitor shock waves and tsunami when an earthquake occurs.

Warnings are given by the Warning Centre if the magnitude of an earthquake is 6.5 or greater on the Richter scale.

Tide stations monitor the arrival of the tsunami waves and transmit information to the Warning Centre.

Tsunami waves destroyed boats and buildings in the harbour area of Kodiak following an earthquake in Alaska in 1964.

Monitoring earthquakes and eruptions

Millions of people around the world live on the slopes of active volcanoes or near active fault zones. It is impossible to prevent earthquakes or eruptions from occurring, but scientists are developing ways of monitoring faults and volcanoes in order to predict when an eruption or earthquake may take place.

Surface monitoring

Before an earthquake or volcanic eruption takes place, changes may occur in the level or shape of the ground. These changes are caused by stress building up in rock at a fault or by magma rising into a magma reservoir within a volcano. Surface movements are monitored using a variety of sensitive instruments, such as tiltmeters, which can detect minute changes in the level of the ground.

Trembling volcanoes

Continuous movement of the ground, known as volcanic tremor, is often recorded on seismometers, days or weeks before a volcano erupts. It is also recorded during an eruption. Tremor is probably caused by magma or gas moving inside a volcano.

Volcanic earthquakes are sometimes felt just before a volcano erupts. When magma rises into a magma reservoir (see page 16),

pressure builds up as its volume increases. This causes stress to build up in the rock surrounding the reservoir. As the stress increases the rock fractures and cracks, and earthquakes occur. Volcanic tremor and earthquakes often indicate that an eruption may be about to take place.

Volcanic tremor is recorded as magma rises into a reservoir.

As pressure builds up, the rock surrounding the reservoir cracks, producing volcanic earthquakes.

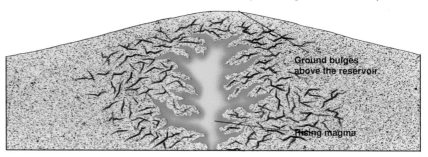

Ground bulges above the reservoir.

Rising magma

Bulge

In 1980, scientists monitoring the volcano Mount St. Helens noticed that the surface was swelling on one side. Instruments were set up to record these ground movements.

The instruments recorded ground movements which showed that the bulge was swelling at a rate of 1.5m (5ft) per day. Volcanologists thought that magma was rising within the volcano.

The bulge grew 90m (295ft) high before a massive eruption took place. Much of the side of the volcano was blasted away, covering the surrounding area with a thick layer of volcanic ash.

Lasers

One method of surface monitoring, known as electronic distance measurement, uses lasers to measure changes in the ground at a fault or on the slope of a volcano. A laser beam from a laser-ranging instrument is aimed at a reflector some distance away. The light is reflected back and the distance that the laser beam travels is calculated by a small computer. The calculations are based on the time taken for the laser beam to travel the distance between

the ranging instrument and the reflector. Over a distance of 1km (3280ft) a change of 1mm (0.04in) in the level of ground can be detected by the instrument.

Lasers are also used to monitor active fault zones. They can detect small movements of the surface along a fault.

Electronic distance measurement instruments are placed far apart on the slope of a volcano.

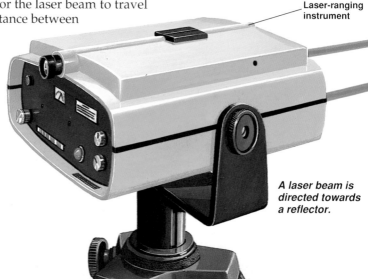

Laser-ranging instrument

A laser beam is directed towards a reflector.

Satellite monitoring

Information from satellites which orbit the Earth is used to monitor volcanoes. Changes in the temperature of the Earth's surface can be detected as magma rises inside a volcano. Ash clouds and gases given off by erupting volcanoes can also be monitored.

Sensors on the satellites detect the intensity of reflected heat or light. This information is transmitted to processing stations where it is converted into a picture of the Earth's surface.

A satellite image of the area surrounding Mount Vesuvius in Italy. The red area around the cone shows a lava flow from its last eruption in 1944.

Seismic gaps

Stress builds up in the rocks along a plate boundary because of the continual movement of the Earth's plates (see pages 6-7). When stress is released, the whole boundary doesn't slip at the same time. Instead, stress is released as sections of the boundary move at different times. By monitoring faults, scientists have discovered that the most likely place for an earthquake to occur is at a section of a fault which has remained stationary for the longest period. They call these sections seismic gaps.

By identifying seismic gaps, scientists are able to select areas of faults to monitor closely.

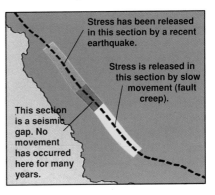

Stress has been released in this section by a recent earthquake.

Stress is released in this section by slow movement (fault creep).

This section is a seismic gap. No movement has occurred here for many years.

Animal warnings

Before some earthquakes, animals have been reported to behave strangely. It is thought that they can sense when an earthquake is about to occur. Scientists think that animals can detect vibrations or changes in electrical currents in rocks which occur before an earthquake. In high risk areas of China, people have been asked to alert scientists if they see animals behaving unusually.

A large earthquake occurred in Haicheng in China in 1975. Before the earthquake, hibernating snakes emerged from underground, despite freezing weather.

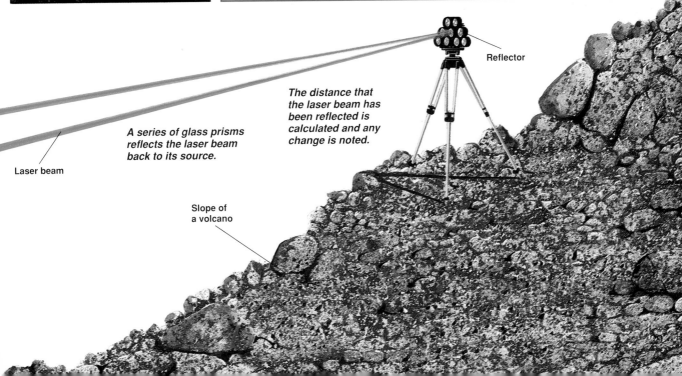

Reflector

The distance that the laser beam has been reflected is calculated and any change is noted.

A series of glass prisms reflects the laser beam back to its source.

Laser beam

Slope of a volcano

Avoiding disasters

Some earthquakes and eruptions can cause great destruction in just a few minutes. Nothing can be done to stop them from occurring, but efforts are being made to reduce their effect and the amount of damage they cause.

Diverting lava-flows

Despite the danger, many people live and work on the slopes of active volcanoes, because volcanic ash contains minerals which make soil very fertile and therefore good for farming. During recent eruptions, attempts have been made to protect towns which are threatened by lava-flows. When Mount Etna erupted in 1992, lava flowed toward the village of Zafferana. Different methods were used to try to stop the lava-flow. Explosives were used in an attempt to break up the lava and huge banks of rocks were built across its path. It was eventually diverted when massive blocks of concrete were lowered onto the lava-flow.

During an eruption of Etna, molten lava flowed through a natural channel beneath solidified lava.

Explosives were used to blast a hole to reach the lava. Concrete blocks were lowered into the lava which blocked the channel and diverted the flow.

Safe buildings

Many cities which lie on active fault zones have laws which require new buildings to be designed and built in a way which will prevent them from collapsing during an earthquake.

Although models of buildings and materials are tested to see how they withstand the effect of an earthquake, it is only when an earthquake occurs that architects are able to see whether their designs are successful. For example, the foundations of some buildings are built to absorb ground movements and reduce the effect of shaking. Some buildings have specially-designed steel frames, joined in such a way that the building sways but does not collapse when the ground shakes.

In Tokyo, in Japan, all new buildings have to be designed to withstand earthquakes.

The new Tokyo City Hall is specially designed to withstand severe shaking.

Inside the concrete walls, a huge framework of of steel strengthens the towers and supports each floor.

Steel framework

Hazard maps

In order to try to predict the effect of an eruption on the area surrounding an active volcano, scientists produce maps, called hazard maps. These show the areas which are likely to be in danger during an eruption from a particular type of hazard, such as a lava-flow or mudflow. When a volcano shows signs of erupting (see pages 28-29), people who live in threatened areas can be evacuated.

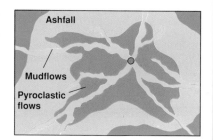

Ashfall

Mudflows

Pyroclastic flows

An example of a hazard map, showing areas which are likely to be in danger during an eruption.

Glossary

Aa. A type of **lava** which has a rough, jagged surface when it solidifies.

Aftershocks. Small earthquakes and tremors which occur as rock resettles after a main earthquake.

Ash. (see **volcanic ash**).

Asthenosphere. A layer of the Earth within the **mantle**. It is thought to consist of partly-melted rock.

Basalt. A dark volcanic rock which is formed when **lava** cools.

Core. The central part of the Earth, below the **mantle**. It is divided into the outer core, which is molten, and the inner core, which is thought to be solid.

Crater. The deep hollow found around the **vents** of some volcanoes.

Crust. The solid, outer layer of the Earth.

Epicentre. A point on the Earth's surface, directly above the **focus** of an earthquake.

Fault. A fracture, or crack, in rocks, along which movement has taken place.

Fault creep. Slow, gradual movement which takes place along a **fault**, without creating earthquakes.

Focus. A point on a **fault** which breaks, causing an earthquake.

Fumarole. A small opening in the ground, from which volcanic gases are given out.

Geothermal energy. Heat energy from inside the Earth, sometimes used for generating electricity.

Geyser. A fountain of hot water and steam, formed from water which has been heated by hot rocks beneath the ground.

Groundwater. Rain or sea water which has seeped into the ground through cracks or tiny spaces between rock particles.

Hot spot. A region where heat rises through the **mantle** and "burns" its way through the **crust**, creating volcanoes on the Earth's surface.

Hot spring. An area of hot water which has risen to the Earth's surface (on land or underwater) after being heated by hot rocks beneath the ground.

Hydrothermal vent. An opening often at **spreading ridges** where heated water, rich in minerals, emerges into cold ocean water.

Island arc. A line of volcanic islands formed near a **plate boundary**, where two plates are moving together.

Lahar (also called a **volcanic mudflow**). A mixture of **volcanic ash** and rocks, melted ice and snow, which flows down a volcano following an eruption.

Lava. The name given to **magma** once it has emerged onto the Earth's surface.

Lava-flow. A stream of molten rock which travels downhill from a **vent** of a volcano during some eruptions.

Lava fountain. A jet of runny **lava**, flung into the air by the pressure of volcanic gases which build up within the **crust**.

Liquefaction. A process which occurs as earthquake shock waves shake wet sand, mud and soil (sediments) causing it to become very mushy.

Lithosphere. A solid layer of the Earth, consisting of the **crust** and the top part of the **mantle**. The lithosphere is broken up into several massive pieces which form the Earth's **plates**.

Magma. Molten (melted) rock inside the Earth, mainly consisting of melted minerals, dissolved gases and water.

Magma chamber. See **Magma reservoir**.

Magma reservoir (also called a **magma chamber**). An area beneath a volcano, where **magma** accumulates.

Mantle. The largest layer of the Earth between the **crust** and the **core**, consisting of the lower **mantle**, the **asthenosphere** and part of the **lithosphere**.

Mercalli scale. A scale based mostly on eyewitness accounts, used to measure the intensity or amount of shaking which occurs at specific places during an earthquake.

Mineral. A natural substance with a specific chemical composition, which does not come from animals or plants. Mineral particles join together to form rocks.

Mudflow (volcanic). See **Lahar**.

Nuée ardente. See **Pyroclastic flow**.

Ocean trench. A very deep undersea valley formed at a **plate boundary** where two plates are moving together and one descends beneath the other.

Pahoehoe. A type of lava which forms a lava-flow with a smooth or wrinkled surface.

Pillow lava. **Lava** which solidifies to resemble pillows. The shapes are formed as lava erupts into water and is cooled quickly.

Plate. One of the several vast areas of **lithosphere** that fit together to form the surface of the Earth.

Plate boundary (also called a **plate margin**). The edge of a **plate**, and are areas where most earthquakes occur and most volcanoes are found.

Plate margin. See **Plate boundary**.

Plate tectonics. All the processes involved when **plates** move across the **asthenosphere**, changing the position, size and shape of continents and oceans.

Pyroclasts. Fragments of rock, **lava** and **volcanic ash** blasted from a volcano during an explosive eruption.

Pyroclastic flow (also called a **nuée ardente**). A cloud of extremely hot gas and **volcanic ash**, which travels at high speed down the slope of an erupting volcano.

Richter scale. A scale used to measure the magnitude, or amount of energy released by an earthquake.

Sea-floor spreading. The process by which oceans widen as **plates** move apart beneath an ocean and **magma** rises to form new ocean floor at a **spreading ridge**.

Sediments. Rock debris, such as sand and mud, which is formed and deposited by the action of wind, water or ice.

Seismic waves. Shock waves which travel from the **focus** of an earthquake in all directions through the Earth.

Spreading ridge. A range of volcanoes, formed on an ocean floor at the boundary of two **plates** which are moving apart during the process of **sea-floor spreading** .

Subduction zone. A **plate boundary** where one plate descends beneath another plate.

Tsunami. A series of massive ocean waves which are created when a large earthquake or a volcanic eruption occurs beneath or close to the sea.

Vent. An opening on the Earth's surface through which **magma**, volcanic gases or steam erupts.

Volcanic ash. Very fine particles of rock and **lava**, formed during explosive eruptions.

Volcanic mudflow. See **Lahar**.

Index

Acknowledgements

Page 7: photo of Alvin © Woods Hole Oceanographic Institution/Rod Catanach
Page 15: photomicrograph of a section of olivine basalt © The Natural History Museum, London.
Page 19: satellite image of a volcanic ash plume from Mount Pinatubo © Robert M. Carey/Science Photo Library
Page 29: satellite image of the Bay of Naples and Mount Vesuvius © NRSC Ltd/ Science Photo Library

The publishers are grateful to the following people and organizations for provision of information and materials for use as artist's reference:
British Geological Survey, Center for Earthquake Studies (Southeast Missouri State University), Patrick Downing, International Tsunami Information Center, Kajima Corporation, Mount St. Helens Visitors Center, Dr John Murray, Nikken Sekkei, Steve Saunders, United States Geological Survey, World Organization of Volcano Observatories.